EVERLASTING ECHOES

A STORY OF LOVE, LOSS AND LEGACY

MAYBE MANDIVAVA

Everlasting Echoes: **A Story Of Love, Loss And Legacy**

Copyright © Maybe Mandivava, 2025

ISBN: 978-1-77928-054-1

Formatted by: Phoenix Publishing

Developmental Editing by: Simbarashe G Masilaha

CONTENTS

DEDICATION

To my daughter precious jewel, Tanyaradzwa Mia Dee, thank you for being my pillar of strength and hope.

To Dee, this book is a heartfelt tribute to your memory, legacy and the profound impact you have had on my life.

ACKNOWLEDGEMENTS

First and foremost, I thank God, whose grace carried me through the darkest valleys and gave me the strength to turn my pain into purpose.

To my beloved Dee, though you are no longer here in body, your love remains everlasting. This book is a tribute to you, our love, and the legacy you left behind.

To my precious daughter, you are my greatest blessing. Your laughter, and endless love remind me daily that joy can be found even after loss.

To my family, my mom, my sisters, my brothers and friends who stood by me when the weight of grief felt unbearable, thank you for your prayers, your kindness, and your unwavering support.

I am deeply grateful for the unwavering support of my pastors during some of my most challenging moments. Despite the strict rules and regulations of the COVID period, Pastors Mr and Mrs Jinjika constantly found time to visit me, offering heartfelt counselling, prayers and his steadfast presence. I also extend my sincere thanks to Bishop Mr Mutume and Mrs Mutume whose prayers and encouragement provided me with strength. I cherish the support from the church members, their prayers, genuine can were truly awesome, reminding me that I was never alone in my journey.

To those who helped bring this book to life, BaChloe and the many voices that encouraged me to share my truth, this would not have been possible without you.

Finally, to every widow, single parent, and grieving heart that picks up this book, may you find solace in knowing that you are not alone. You are strong, capable, and worthy of love and happiness.

1

WHERE IT ALL BEGAN

L ove is a peculiar thing, a force that defies logic and reason, a sensation that wraps itself around your heart like a vine, creeping into the crevices of your soul until it becomes impossible to untangle.

Falling in love is even stranger, like stepping into a dream you didn't know you were dreaming. How does one describe the indescribable? How do you put into words the first flicker of love's flame, the way it dances in the dark, casting shadows and light in equal measure? Love is not meant to be confined to language, for words are too clumsy, too finite, to capture its infinite essence. To describe love is to try to hold water in your hands—it slips through your fingers, leaving only the memory of its coolness behind.

I was not searching for love when I walked through the doors of ZB Bank's Masvingo Branch in February 2019. Love was the farthest thing from my mind. I was there for a job, for the experience, for the steady income that would allow me to stand on my own two feet. Love? Love was a luxury I could not afford, a distraction I did not need. I was new to the banking world, green and untested, and I knew that if I were to survive, I would have to learn quickly. Money, after all, is a serious matter. People do not take kindly to mistakes when it comes to their hard-earned cash.

I was assigned a mentor, a man named Dee. He was a seasoned veteran in the banking industry, a man whose reputation preceded him. He was respected, admired, and, if I'm being honest, a little intimidating. His demeanour was one of quiet authority, the kind of man who could silence a room with a single glance. I was nervous, acutely aware of my inexperience, and terrified of making a mistake that would reflect poorly on him. Looking back, I realize now that my fear of disappointing him outweighed my fear of failing at the job itself. Perhaps he sensed my apprehension, because over time, his stern exterior softened. He became patient, kind, and unexpectedly gentle in his guidance. His patience put me at ease, and under his tutelage, I began to find my footing.

I threw myself into my work with a determination that surprised even me. I have always been someone who thrives on challenges, who sees obstacles not as roadblocks but as puzzles waiting to be solved. Banking was no different. The intricacies of the job, the numbers, the transactions, the clients—it all fascinated me. Before long, I had mastered the rhythm of the workplace, navigating its complexities with a confidence that belied my newness. Dee watched my progress with a quiet pride, and I, in turn, felt a sense of accomplishment that was both foreign and exhilarating.

As the weeks turned into months, I became an integral part of the team. I formed connections with my colleagues, built friendships, and found a sense of belonging that I hadn't realized I was missing. Dee and I, too, grew closer. What began as a professional relationship slowly evolved into a friendship, one built on mutual respect and a shared dedication to our work. We spent hours together, discussing clients, transactions, and the nuances of banking. But as the days passed, our conversations began to stray beyond the confines of work.

One day, I found myself opening up to him about my life outside the bank. I told him that I wasn't looking for love, and that I was content to focus on my career and let the chips fall where they may. He nodded in understanding, revealing that he felt the same way. His last relationship, he said, had left him numb, his heart hardened by the pain of betrayal. He didn't go into details, and I didn't press him. I, too, had my share of heartbreak, though my experiences were less dramatic, more a series of misadventures than a single, defining tragedy.

Our shared disinterest in love created an unspoken bond between us, a sense of camaraderie that made it easier to relax in each other's presence. I told myself that there was no risk of romantic entanglement, that we were simply two people who understood each other. But life, as it often does, had other plans.

On April 4, 2019, one of Dee's friends hosted a birthday party at Wimpy in Masvingo. I was invited, along with several of my colleagues. I was hesitant at first—I hadn't yet fully settled into the social dynamics of the workplace—but I decided to go. It was an opportunity to step out of my comfort zone, to see my co-workers in a different light. The office, after all, has a way of masking people's true selves, of reducing them to their roles and responsibilities. But outside of work, in the carefree atmosphere of a party, people reveal themselves in ways that are often surprising.

The party was lively, the air thick with laughter and the clinking of glasses. Colleagues who were usually reserved and professional had transformed into social butterflies, their inhibitions loosened by the flow of alcohol and the absence of workplace formalities. I found myself enjoying the moment, caught up in the energy of the room. I was deep in conversation with a co-worker when my eyes wandered across the room and landed on Dee.

He was, as always, impeccably dressed, his style a perfect blend of casual and refined. He wore a smart shirt and well-fitted trousers, the kind of outfit that spoke of effortless sophistication. He must have felt my gaze, because without turning his head, he cast me a sidelong glance, a hint of a smile playing on his lips. I felt a flutter in my chest, a sensation I quickly brushed aside.

But then, as if drawn by some invisible force, I turned my head and found him looking at me. His eyes locked onto mine, and for a moment, the noise of the party faded into the background. I felt warmth spread across my face, a blush creeping up my cheeks. He began to walk toward me, his smile widening with each step. As he approached, I noticed something I hadn't before—dimples. How had I never noticed those dimples?

When he reached me, there was a brief moment of awkwardness. We had spoken countless times before, but always within the context of work. Our conversations had been easy, but they had always been anchored in the safe territory of banking. Here, in this unfamiliar setting, there was no work to retreat to, no familiar ground to stand on.

"It's a fine evening," he said finally, breaking the silence. "Are you enjoying yourself?"

I smiled and told him I was.

"People need to go out sometimes," he added, his voice carrying a hint of something I couldn't quite place. "Escape the strain of work."

There was a tension in the air between us, a shift in the dynamic that I hadn't noticed before. Maybe it was the change of environment, or maybe it was something else entirely.

As the night wore on, the ice between us melted. For the first time, we spoke without the invisible barrier of work between us. We talked about our dreams, our aspirations, the things that made us who we were. It was refreshing, a glimpse into a side of him I had never seen before.

That night, something unexpected happened. A feeling stirred within me, one I had not experienced in a long time. It was a strange yet familiar sensation, a connection that went beyond words. I felt myself being drawn toward emotions I had not welcomed for some time. Warmth spread through me, my heart quickening in a way I barely recognized.

By the end of the night, he looked at me and said something I hadn't expected. "You've changed my perception of women," he admitted. "You would make a good wife."

The words caught me off guard. I blushed, feeling my resolve melt in a way that almost embarrassed me. But what struck me most was not just what he said, but how he said it. He wasn't flirting—at least, it didn't feel like he was. His voice was sincere, an honesty that unsettled me in the best way possible.

We exchanged numbers that night, something that, in hindsight, seemed long overdue. What started as hesitant WhatsApp conversations soon took a more personal turn. The exchanges were awkward at first, but gradually, the formality between us began to dissolve. He mentioned that his birthday was on April 8th and casually invited me to another party.

Somewhere along the way, our conversations shifted. The professionalism that once defined our interactions gave way to something softer, more playful. Our chats became less about bank transactions and more about each other. There was an undeniable shift, a transition that felt both thrilling and unsettling.

I found myself drawn to the way he balanced it all, how he could be flirtatious one moment and effortlessly slip back into his role at work. Sometimes, we would exchange secret smiles across the office, and each time, a flicker of guilt stirred within me. It both thrilled and unnerved me, challenging the principles I had always held so firmly.

I was scared because I was letting my guard down. I was scared because I didn't know how I had ended up under the spell of this man's hypnotizing charm. I was used to being in control of every conversation, guarding against stirring up any emotions and desires. I wasn't looking for it, after all.

When the day of his birthday celebrations arrived, I carefully dressed up and made my way to the party. I hated to admit it, even to myself, but I had chosen my outfit with someone in mind— Dee. The realization unsettled me. I didn't want to acknowledge the effect he was beginning to have on my thoughts, my actions, and my everyday life. Yet there I was, suddenly conscious of how I walked, how I laughed, how I presented myself, all because he would be there.

The party was alive with energy, an electrifying atmosphere buzzing in the air. I quickly spotted Dee, looking effortlessly suave and debonair. Summoning my courage, I approached him. My heart pounded, and to my surprise, my palms were damp with nervous sweat. He noticed me immediately. For a fleeting second, I saw his face light up, but then, as if catching himself, he masked his reaction, composing his expression into something more neutral, feigning only mild interest in my presence.

That night, it turned out that he had been hoping I would come. He had been waiting for me. Months later, during one of our light-hearted moments, he would deny it with playful defiance. But I held my ground, insisting that on that day, he had been eagerly anticipating my arrival. I would even exaggerate, teasing that he had probably whispered a silent prayer that I wouldn't change my mind at the last minute. It became an ongoing joke between us, one that always ended in laughter.

That night, we talked about almost everything, losing ourselves in a world of our own, untouched by the noise of the celebration around us. We spoke of life as it was and as we wished it to be, of realities and dreams until the boundary between the two seemed to blur. Our hopes and aspirations intertwined so seamlessly that it became impossible to separate his from mine. There was laughter, the kind that came effortlessly, and smiles that lingered a little too long. Somewhere in the midst of it all, we both felt it, that quiet realization that we had ventured too far for two people who weren't looking for love. We were teetering on the edge of something unspoken, something neither of us had planned for. And yet, we let ourselves slip, unguarded, unafraid.

The initial shyness had vanished. It no longer felt awkward to hold each other's gaze. The hesitation that once existed had melted away, replaced by a quiet certainty. And in that moment, I could no longer deny it—I was falling for him.

Late that night, we reached a point where words no longer sufficed. The unspoken connection between us had woven its magic, rendering language useless. We simply stood there, locked in each other's gaze, as if caught in a trance—two souls spellbound by a force neither of us fully understood.

Then, he stepped closer, his movements slow, deliberate. Gently, he pulled me in and pressed his lips against mine. In that moment, that night, the stars—I dared to believe it—twinkled in quiet wonder. I had surrendered. The walls I had so carefully built crumbled in an instant, and I let myself fall for him, for us, for whatever lay ahead.

It was the beginning of forever.

The journey had begun, like the first light of dawn breaking over the horizon, tender and tentative, yet brimming with the promise of what was to come. It was a journey that would unravel the tightly wound threads of my heart, threads I had knotted and tucked away, vowing never to let them flutter freely again. But life, in its infinite wisdom, has a way of rewriting the stories we tell ourselves, of painting over the lines we draw in the sand. And so, when Dee stepped into my life, he did not merely cross those lines—he erased them entirely, leaving behind a blank canvas upon which a new story would be written.

From the moment I allowed him into my world, the air around me seemed to shimmer with a new kind of energy. It was as if the universe itself had shifted, aligning the stars to guide me toward a love I had sworn I would never again embrace. I had built walls around my heart, high and impenetrable, fortified by the scars of past hurts. But Dee, with his gentle persistence and unwavering kindness, did not storm those walls. Instead, he whispered to them, softly and patiently, until they crumbled of their own accord. And there I stood, exposed and vulnerable, yet somehow unafraid.

He was impossible not to love, this man who carried himself with a quiet confidence, who gave without expectation and loved without reservation. He was a giver, not just of material things—though he delighted in surprising me with chocolates that melted on my tongue, jewellery that sparkled like captured starlight, and handwritten cards that bore the weight of his heart—but of himself. He gave me his time, his attention, his laughter, and his dreams. And in doing so, he awakened something within me that I had thought long buried: the belief in love's power to heal, to transform, to make whole what had been broken.

Days turned into weeks, and weeks into months, each one a brushstroke on the canvas of our shared life. I found myself changing, growing, and becoming someone I had not been in a very long time. At work, I carried myself differently, my steps lighter, my smile more frequent. I was no longer just a woman going through the motions of life; I was a woman alive with purpose, with joy, with love. Dee's presence in my life was like a steady flame, warming me from the inside out, illuminating the corners of my soul that had long been shrouded in darkness.

Our love was not without its challenges. When I was transferred to ZB Bank's Harare branch, leaving behind the familiar streets of Masvingo, the distance between us could have been a chasm. But we bridged it with determination and trust, taking turns to travel to each other on weekends. Dee would deposit money into my account, not because he had to, but because he wanted to taste my cooking, to savour the fried rice, sticky wings, and fish that I prepared with love. And I, in turn, cherished those moments, the way his eyes lit up when he took the first bite, the way his laughter filled the room, the way his presence made even the simplest of meals feel like a feast.

Distance, they say, weakens love. But for us, it only made it stronger. Our bond was built on a foundation of mutual trust and understanding, a foundation so solid that not even the miles between us could shake it. Knowing that we had something so rare and so precious filled me with a quiet contentment, a happiness that was not loud or boastful, but steady and sure, like the beating of my own heart.

December 2020 arrived, a month that would change everything. We had been together for over a year, weathering the storms of life with an ease that made it seem effortless. Dee invited me to spend Christmas with him, promising a gift that he refused to reveal, no matter how much I pleaded or prodded. The anticipation was almost unbearable, my mind spinning with fantasies, each one more elaborate than the last. What could it be? What could he possibly give me that would match the depth of my love for him?

Christmas Day arrived, and still, he kept his secret, insisting that I wait until Boxing Day to open my gift. The hours dragged on, each one stretching into an eternity, until finally, the moment came. He handed me a big red box, its wrapping paper gleaming under the soft glow of the lights. My hands trembled as I tore through it, my heart racing with excitement. But then, I felt it—a shift in the air, a heaviness that made my breath catch in my throat. I looked up, and there he was, kneeling before me, holding a small box in his hands.

Inside was a ring, a silver double ring adorned with sparkling stones that caught the light and refracted it into a thousand tiny rainbows. He asked me a question, his voice steady but filled with emotion, and for a moment, I could not process it. Was this real? Was he really asking me to marry him? The world seemed to tilt on its axis, everything narrowing down to this one moment, this one man, and this one question.

And then it hit me, a wave of emotions so powerful that it threatened to sweep me away. Tears rose from deep within me, spilling over and cascading down my cheeks in a torrent that I could not stop. I felt joy, disbelief, gratitude, and love, all swirling together in a kaleidoscope of feelings that left me breathless. Without thinking, I leaped into his arms, hugging him so tightly that I almost squeezed the air out of him. We were locked in a fierce, intimate embrace, consumed by a love that was as deep as it was unshakable.

This was it. This was the culmination of everything we had been through, the trials and the triumphs, the laughter and the tears. We were engaged. I was now his fiancée, and he was my future. He had shown me, in every possible way, how committed he was to me, and I no longer wanted to waste any more time before building a life with him.

On New Year's Eve, we celebrated with friends at Caravan Park in Masvingo, a place where the air was filled with laughter and the promise of new beginnings. As the clock struck midnight, marking the start of 2021, I felt a strange sensation, a nagging thought that perhaps my happiness was too great, that the universe might demand a price for it. But I quickly dismissed the thought, refusing to let fear taint the future that lay ahead. This was my year, our year, and I was determined to shape it with love and hope.

We made our plans, eager and impatient. We would marry that year, he would pay my lobola, and I would become his wife in every sense of the word. And then, a few months later, I discovered that I was pregnant. The news filled us with a joy so profound that it seemed to overflow, spilling into every corner of our lives. We decided to accelerate our plans, eager to move forward before my bump became noticeable.

One day, we took a trip to visit our potential wedding venue, the Great Zimbabwe Hotel in Masvingo. We drove there with his close friends, the air filled with excitement and anticipation. The venue was beautiful, a place where our dreams could take root and flourish. We gathered all the information we needed, each step bringing us closer to the life we were building together. It was a joyful time, a time of relishing the moment and the path we were creating.

We scheduled the 3rd of July 2021 as our lobola day, and we put everything in place for the big occasion. The house where the negotiations would take place was decorated to perfection, every detail carefully considered. The day brought with it an overwhelming sense of happiness and fulfilment. I will never forget the message Dee sent me that morning: "This is the day that the Lord has made! We will rejoice and be glad in it! First steps towards the beginning of a new era for US! Besty turned wifey." It was a beautiful reminder that we had finally made it.

Dee and his entourage arrived, looking sharp and confident. He wore brown chino trousers paired with a traditional-themed shirt adorned with golden floral pockets, perfectly matching the lower part of my dress. When we stood together for our photos, we looked like we belonged, perfectly in sync, two halves of a whole. The ceremony unfolded smoothly, and as the day drew to a close, I felt an overwhelming gratitude to God. I was left speechless, my emotions running deep. I wanted to cry and laugh all at once, but the joy in my heart would not let me. I was so nervous the entire day, that same feeling I had at the start of the year. But this time, I chose to focus on the happiness of the moment and stay positive.

Dee was finally my husband. I felt like the luckiest woman in the world, and with every fibre of my being, I loved him more than ever before. Our journey had begun, and though I did not know what the future held, I knew that as long as we were together, we could face anything. For love, true love, is not just a feeling—it is a promise, a commitment, a journey that we take together, hand in hand, heart in heart.

2

SHATTERED DREAMS

L ife has a way of surprising us when we least expect it, often in the cruellest of ways. For me, the surprise came in the form of a whirlwind of emotions that began with the happiest day of my life—my traditional marriage. That day, my world transformed, and a new sense of hope blossomed within me. I believed that my life had found a deeper meaning, anchored in the love I had discovered. There was no doubt in my heart that Dee loved me. It felt as though he had been created to love me, and only me.

The first week after our marriage felt like a dream, almost too perfect to be real. I revelled in the bliss of knowing that I belonged to someone, and I was adjusting to calling Dee my husband. The transition was both awkward and exhilarating, like a baby learning to walk for the first time. Dee shared in the excitement, too. I was carrying his child, and he was soon to be a father. He even began calling himself *Baba* (Father), with a sense of pride and joy that made my heart swell.

But it was just two weeks and three days into this fantasy that tragedy struck. Everything had been calm, sweet, and hopeful when Dee contracted COVID-19. He was quickly admitted to a local private hospital in Masvingo. Though the disease had become a global pandemic and claimed many lives, I was hopeful—no, certain—that he would recover. My faith was strong, and so was his. We were going to get through this together. I had travelled from work to be with him, even though they had told me he had COVID. I could not bear to stay away from him. I needed to be there for him, and the thought of contracting the virus never crossed my mind. I visited him regularly, bringing his favourite meals to the hospital, taking care of everything he needed as his wife—making sure he was warm, had a change of clothes, and was as comfortable as possible in the sterile, clinical environment.

It was around 5:20 AM on the 20th of July, 2021, when I received the phone call that changed my entire life. The call came like a thunderclap, its words feeling like a knife twisting in my chest—a piercing pain that left my heart shattered into a million pieces. My aunt, Dee's sister, was on the other end, and her words—"Your husband passed away around 0400 when he got worse in the hospital"—echoed in my mind, but I could not comprehend them. I could not believe it. I felt like I was trapped in a nightmare I could not wake up from. I jumped out of bed, my heart racing, and ran to my mother's room, which was at the far end of the house. "Mom, call her back now! Tell them it's not true! It can't be true!" I screamed.

But the news hit me like a tidal wave when my mother confirmed it, crashing over me with such painful clarity that it felt like the ground had disappeared beneath me. The world stood still as the weight of the grief pulled me down. My heart felt like it was breaking into a million jagged pieces, and I could not breathe. I ran around the house, hysterical, screaming, and desperate for my mother to open the gate so I could run to the hospital. It was not far, but in that moment, it felt like it was miles away.

We rushed to the hospital, clinging to a shred of hope that maybe, somehow, this was all a mistake. My mind was racing with the thought of him, of seeing him, of holding his hand, of hearing his voice. But when we got there, the staff would not let me in. They said it was for my safety, but their words did not matter to me. It was a hollow excuse. I could not hear them. I ran to the other side of the building, knowing there was no entrance, but I had spotted a window, small and distant during my hospital visits. I pressed my face against it, desperate to see him, even if I could not make out a thing. I needed to see him just one last time.

At that moment, all I wanted to do was scream and cry, to find some way to release the unbearable pain that was consuming me. But instead, I went numb, broken, as the words from the hospital staff that he was gone sank in. The wave of disbelief crashed over me, and I could not make sense of it. How could this be happening? How could he be gone when we had just started our beautiful journey together? I was left reeling, asking myself, questioning everything—how could this be real? How could life be so cruel? You even find yourself questioning God in moments like these, wondering why this was happening.

The future we had dreamed of was ripped away in the blink of an eye. All the congratulations I had received from friends and family just days before now turned into condolences. As I write this now, I can still hear the echoes of my screams, calling out for help, searching for answers that no one could give.

I felt emptiness so deep; it consumed me in a way that words could never capture. Every inch of the house felt like a reminder of the pain, and I had nowhere to turn. I collapsed to my knees, crying out, calling for anyone I could find, even strangers, begging them to come and see what had happened to me. I can still remember when my Pastor arrived. In my grief, I touched his feet, crying uncontrollably, and I asked him, "Is this how your God works? What kind of God do we worship? A good God who gives you something today and takes it away tomorrow? Is this the God who gives with one hand and takes with the other? Why did our God allow this to happen, knowing it would not last?" I asked him a barrage of questions, but all I remember was him laying his hands on my head and praying for me. His words felt distant, almost as if they could not reach the brokenness inside me.

I was spiralling into a storm of emotions, each wave threatening to tear apart whatever was left of my sanity. One moment stood out so vividly in my mind when I screamed at the top of my lungs, "Ko mwana?" (What about the baby?). That was when my family realized I was pregnant. We had decided to keep it to ourselves. In the chaos of grief, it felt as though I had forgotten about the pregnancy. I had forgotten that a child was growing inside me. I lost track of time, losing consciousness again and again that day, swept away in a whirlwind of sorrow and disbelief.

Before I could even begin to process the enormity of my grief, I was told that my husband would be buried the next day in Kwekwe, Zimbabwe. Due to COVID-19 regulations, in Zimbabwe, burials had to happen within 24-48 hours, to minimize the risk of transmission. Everything felt like it was happening too fast, too soon. I had just spoken to him on the phone after midnight on the 20th of July, telling me he was fighting just fine and that I should not worry too much about him, and only four hours later, I was told he was dead and would be buried in less than a day. My mind could not comprehend the rush, the shock— it was all too overwhelming. And if that was not enough, I was told there would be no viewing of his body.

When I thought about death before, it always seemed like a final, absolute end, something painful but inevitable. I never understood the weight people placed on viewing a loved one's body, thinking it was just part of the grieving process, a formality that did not change the reality of loss. But when death comes for someone you love in its most ruthless and unrelenting form, it does not just take them—it shatters every belief you once held. It strips away logic and reason, leaving only raw, unbearable grief in its place.

The cruellest part of losing someone to COVID-19 was the denial of a final goodbye. No body viewing, no quiet moment to stand beside him, to touch his hand one last time, to make peace with the reality of his passing. COVID-19 robbed us of closure, forcing us to grieve without proof, without the solemn ritual of farewell. It left so many of us trapped in a spiral of unanswered questions and unresolved emotions, making it even harder to accept what had happened.

I had wanted Dee to wear the suit I bought him for his 31st birthday, his last birthday, a gift he had loved, a symbol of the life and love we had shared. I needed to see him, to make sense of it, to truly believe he was gone. There were things I needed to tell him, questions I desperately wanted to ask, even though I knew he would never answer—but which I believed he would carry in his spirit to the other side. I just wanted to do something, to say something—maybe I would have felt better. I wanted him to know that whatever cruel forces had stolen him from me had been unjust and merciless. I still needed him. How was I supposed to raise our child alone? Every word I uttered came from the depths of my shattered heart, carried on a tide of emotions that spilled from my eyes in relentless torrents of tears.

Death is not just cruel—it is mercilessly final. All I know is I had just changed his clothes the day before this was happening. He was wrapped in the same pyjamas I had bought for him upon his request on Father's Day in 2021, and his feet were covered in the thick socks I had borrowed from my mother to keep him warm. That was it. That was how he was laid to rest.

The last time I had seen his face was on the 19th when I had visited him, never knowing it would be the last. I had no chance to say goodbye. No moment to whisper my love one last time. Now, all I had left were fragments of memories, scattered and distorted by the whirlwind of grief that had overtaken me.

Everything felt rushed, as if the same cruel force that had ripped him away from me swiftly and mercilessly, like an eagle snatching its prey, was determined to erase every trace of him as quickly as possible. He was buried in the morning of the 21st of July 2021. No farewell, no final touch, no moment to honour the love we had shared. In the blink of an eye, my beloved husband had become nothing more than a "diseased corpse" that people wanted to put in the ground as if his presence itself was a threat. Thanks to my brother, who was bold enough and went close to the coffin and took pictures of the wrapped coffin till he was in the soil. Everyone else, we were told to be distant and be close only when the coffin was six feet under the ground. The air was thick with grief, but beneath it, an unmistakable fear lingered. Even among those who knew and loved him, there was a quiet terror—everyone was afraid of being next.

I stood there, frozen in place, as I watched shovels of earth fall relentlessly onto his grave. Each thud echoed through my soul, a cruel finality I could not bear to accept. For a moment, the ground seemed like a monstrous, insatiable beast devouring my husband, swallowing him whole as if he had never existed. A raw, anguished wail tore from my throat, but it did nothing to stop the inevitable. The world was burying him; they were erasing him.

I knew how this would go. People would grieve for a while, murmur his name in hushed voices, and then eventually move on. Life would call them back to its routine, and soon, he would become just a memory to them. But for me, the weight of this loss would never lift. I would carry it, alone, in the deepest chambers of my heart. My family, who had attended the burial with me, tried to comfort me, but their words felt hollow against the magnitude of my grief. Nothing made sense. Nothing could.

After the burial, I visited Dee's parents' home for the first time. It was there that I met his father, a man I had never had the chance to know before. Introductions were made, but everything felt distant, unreal—just another painful formality in a day that had already stolen too much from me. After everything was done, I left with my family. I needed them. The pain was unbearable, and I knew I could not face it alone.

The days that followed were a haze of tears and heartache. I moved through them like a ghost, my body present but my soul elsewhere. I would wake up in the middle of the night, reaching for Dee, only to find his side of the bed cold and empty. I would catch myself listening for his voice, for the sound of his laughter, only to be met with silence. The places, once filled with his presence, now felt like a tomb—a place where memories lingered like shadows, haunting me at every turn. It felt like I was in a daze, aware of the reality around me but unable to fully grasp it. I kept telling myself it was just a nightmare, a terrible dream, and that I would wake up to find Dee lying beside me, smiling like he always did. I fought with every ounce of my being to wake up, to escape this horrid reality. But the more I tried, the more they told me I was in denial. The truth was too much for my mind to accept—that Dee was gone.

I tried to find solace in the baby growing inside me, but even that brought a bittersweet ache. This child, our child, would never know their father. Dee would never hold them, never see their first steps, and never hear their first words. The life we had dreamed of building together was gone, replaced by a future that felt uncertain and lonely.

Grief is a strange and unpredictable companion. Some days, it would wrap itself around me like a heavy blanket, suffocating me with its weight. Other days, it would recede, leaving me with moments of clarity where I could almost convince myself that I was okay. But then, like a wave crashing onto the shore, it would return, pulling me under once more.

I found myself questioning everything—my faith, my purpose, my ability to go on. How could I raise a child alone? How could I face a future without Dee? The questions swirled in my mind, unanswered and unanswerable.

But even in the darkest moments, there were glimmers of light. My family, my friends, and even strangers reached out to me, offering their support and love. They reminded me that I was not alone, that I had people who cared for me and would stand by me no matter what. And there was the baby—a tiny, fragile reminder of the love of Dee that was growing inside my womb. This child was a part of him, a piece of him that would live on. I saw hope— a hope that, despite the pain, life could still be beautiful.

The journey ahead would not be easy. I knew that. But I also knew that I had to keep going, for myself and for our child. Dee may be gone, but his love, his spirit, would always be with me. And in that love, I would find the strength to carry on.

Life had taken so much from me, but it had also given me something precious—a love that had changed me, a love that would never truly die. And so, with a heart that was both broken and full, I took my first steps into a future that was uncertain, but not without hope.

3

THROUGH THE SHADOWS

Grief, that unrelenting thief of joy, had wrapped its cold, skeletal fingers around my heart, squeezing until I could no longer breathe, no longer think, no longer feel. It was a shadow that followed me everywhere, a weight that pressed down on my chest, making each day a battle to simply exist. I had become a hollow shell, a vessel emptied of all that once made me whole.

My appetite had vanished, replaced by a gnawing emptiness that no food could fill. My mind, once sharp and vibrant, had dulled to a foggy haze, and my body, once alive with energy, had turned to stone. I was numb, so numb that I could sit for hours, staring into the void, unblinking, unfeeling, as if I had been hypnotized by some unseen force. Time lost all meaning. Minutes stretched into hours, hours into days, and still, I remained motionless, wide awake yet utterly disconnected from the world around me.

The pain of losing Dee was a wound so deep, so raw, that it defied description. He was my everything—my partner, my confidant, my rock. His laughter had been the melody that filled my days, his touch the warmth that soothed my soul. And now, he was gone. Just like that. The world had lost its colour, its music, and it's light. I was adrift in a sea of sorrow, struggling to find my footing in a life that no longer made sense. And yet, even in the midst of my grief, there was a glimmer of hope, a tiny spark of life growing inside me—our unborn child. But even that hope was tinged with fear, with uncertainty. How could I navigate this new reality without him? How could I raise our child alone, when the very thought of facing each day without him felt like an insurmountable task?

As if the weight of my grief and the burden of my pregnancy were not enough, I found myself entangled in a web of family misunderstandings that only deepened my pain. Dee's death had not only stolen my husband but had also disrupted the fragile process of integrating into his family. I was still in the early stages of building connections with his siblings, trying to foster a sense of belonging, to prove that I was worthy of their love and acceptance. They did not know much about me, and Dee's sudden death had left me in limbo, unsure of where I truly stood with them. I had hoped that they would trust their son, their brother, to know why he had chosen to marry me. I had hoped that they would see me not as an outsider, but as someone who had loved him deeply, someone who was now carrying a piece of him within me.

But hope, as I would soon learn, is a fragile thing, easily shattered by the harsh realities of life. Something happened that shattered what little strength I had left, something that would change everything. Dee's family had begun the process of acquiring his death certificate, and an error at the registry office ignited a storm of tension between us. For reasons I still do not understand, they had intended to record his marital status as "single." However, when the document was issued, it stated that he was "customarily married." And that small, seemingly insignificant detail changed everything.

My father-in-law called me, his voice filled with fury that I could not comprehend. Some of Dee's relatives were enraged, and to my utter shock, they blamed me. They accused me of interfering, of somehow altering the record without their consent. Their anger felt like a dagger to my already bleeding heart. I could not understand why his marital status even mattered at this point, why in the face of such a profound loss, this was what they chose to fixate on. More painfully, I could not comprehend why they wanted to erase the truth of our union. I was blindsided, unprepared for this battle. It was too soon, too raw, too much.

I later discovered that they wanted to register Dee as "single" so they could claim his financial benefits from his workplace. The realization stung, but I could not bring myself to care about money. I had just lost the love of my life, the father of my unborn child. My world had crumbled, and all I wanted was to grieve in peace. I could not understand why they assumed I was after financial gain when my heart was drowning in sorrow. Their accusations were cruel beyond words. They called me a gold digger, insisting that I had only married Dee for his money, waiting to collect once he was gone. Some even went as far as to suggest that I had a hand in his death. That accusation shattered me to my core. What kind of person would kill their husband, choosing to face pregnancy alone, to raise a child without the father they had dreamed of? The mere thought was unbearable.

Until that moment, I had believed that everyone in his family mourned him just as deeply as I did. I had thought we were bound by the same grief, united in our loss. But the day I realized I was at the centre of a storm driven by greed and selfishness, my heart broke all over again. Dee and I had never built our relationship on money; it had been nothing but pure, unwavering love. Even as I carried his child, I had no idea whatsoever how I would survive the months ahead without him. Yet, money was the last thing on my mind. But the insults kept coming, relentless and cruel. They pressured me to sign an affidavit stating that though the death certificate showed that I was married to Dee, I was willing for them to claim his financial benefits from his workplace.

At that point, I was so emotionally drained that I was ready to agree to anything just for them to leave me alone, to let me grieve in peace. What hurt the most was how quickly some of Dee's family had set aside their grief the moment money became involved. I wanted to scream at them, to tell them that I did not care about the money. All I wanted was my husband back so we could build the future we had dreamed of together. I wanted Tanya to grow up with her father, to hear his voice, to feel his love. No amount of money could ever replace that. But it seemed they would never understand.

I even tried to write the affidavit and get it signed, but every commissioner of oaths I approached refused. They were determined to have it signed by someone of their choosing. When I finally confided in my family about what was happening, they strongly advised me against signing anything. The situation became tense, and I could feel tempers rising on both sides. I feared that if I did not handle things wisely, there would be a full-blown conflict between Dee's family and mine. That was the last thing I wanted. I did not want my child to be born into a war between families.

As time passed, the baby bump started to show. I was carrying not only the weight of my grief but also the fragile life growing inside me. The emotional toll was unbearable, and my body began to show signs of distress. I started bleeding and had to undergo a cervical cerclage, also known as a cervical stitch procedure, performed by one of the best doctors in Harare, Zimbabwe. But just a day later, the suture failed. The baby had stopped moving for days, and the doctors were convinced I had miscarried.

My family, devastated by the news, could not find the courage to tell me. Unaware of what they already knew, I went on with my plans. The same day I was scheduled for a dilation and curettage procedure—not knowing it was also the day I had booked a routine pregnancy check-up since the baby was not moving. It was at that appointment that my family learned the unimaginable: the baby was still alive. The only explanation was that the baby had simply not been moving, as they can be like that sometimes. Meanwhile, I had already started taking medication meant for a miscarriage, thinking it was to stop bleeding. The moment my family found out, they told me to stop taking it immediately.

The relief that washed over me was indescribable, but it was short-lived. The emotional rollercoaster had taken its toll, and I was left feeling more fragile than ever. The thought of losing our child, the last piece of Dee I had left, was too much to bear. I clung to the hope that we would make it through, that somehow, against all odds, we would find a way to survive this storm. But deep down, I knew that the road ahead would be long and fraught with challenges. And as I sat there, my hand resting on my growing belly, I whispered a silent prayer for strength, for courage, for the will to keep going, no matter what.

The world has a way of bending and twisting, like a river carving its path through the stubborn earth. It does not ask for permission; it simply flows, carrying with it the weight of joy and sorrow, triumph and despair. And so it was that my life, once steady and predictable, became a torrent of emotions, a cascade of events that would forever alter the landscape of my soul.

It began with my sister's voice, soft yet resolute, as she unravelled the truth to me that they thought I had miscarried as told by professional doctors. Her words were like a key, unlocking a door I had not known existed. And when that door swung open, I stepped into a world where the miraculous and the mundane danced together, where the hand of God was visible in every twist and turn. That experience, that revelation, opened my eyes wide, wider than they had ever been. I saw, for the first time, that His promises were not fragile things, easily shattered by the storms of life. No, they were steadfast, unyielding, untouched by grief, unshaken by high blood pressure, depression, or even the cruellest of medical complications. If a child was meant to be born, no force on earth could prevent it. In that moment, I understood that God was not a man, bound by human limitations. His plans were vast, intricate, and often beyond the reach of my understanding.

I remember the days at work in Borrowdale, the migraines that would descend without warning, sharp and unyielding. I would feel the world tilt, the edges of my vision blur, and then darkness would claim me. I lost count of how many times I fainted, how many times I woke to the concerned faces of my manager, my team, my colleagues. They became my lifeline, my anchors in the storm. They did not judge me, did not turn away from my pain. Instead, they stood by me, their presence a quiet reminder that I was not alone. They walked with me through the valley of depression, anxiety, and grief, their kindness a balm to my wounded spirit.

As the months passed, the due date drew nearer, and with it came complications that no one could have foreseen. My body, weary from the strain, could not wait for the full term. In January 2022, I gave birth to my daughter through a caesarean section. The experience was both terrifying and miraculous, a paradox that left me breathless. She was here, this tiny, fragile being who could not wait nine months to meet me. They placed her in an incubator, her small body tethered to oxygen, and I watched her with a mixture of awe and fear. But then, finally, they handed her to me, and in that moment, the world stood still.

Holding her for the first time, I felt a love so profound, so all-encompassing, that it seemed to erase all the pain that had come before. She was perfect, her tiny fingers curling around mine, her eyes blinking up at me as if to say, "I am here, and I am yours." In her face, I saw so much of Dee, his features etched into hers, a living reminder of the man I had loved and lost. For a moment, it felt as though I was holding a piece of him, a tiny version of the man who had been taken from me too soon. I could not stop smiling, could not stop the tears that flowed freely down my cheeks. I praised God, my heart overflowing with gratitude. She was here, and she was perfect.

I named her Tanyaradzwa, a name that means "God has comforted us." And indeed, she was a comfort, a precious jewel that God had brought into my life for reasons I could not yet fully understand. Every time I looked at her, I felt a joy and strength that I had not known was possible. She became my reason, my purpose, and my light in the darkness. I prayed every day that she would grow to be the best version of herself that she would make me proud, that she would be a better person than I could ever hope to be.

But even as Tanya brought joy into my life, the world outside continued to test me. My father-in-law, a man whose heart seemed hardened by loss and bitterness, did not relent in his onslaught. When Tanya was born, he made it clear that he wanted nothing to do with her. His words were sharp, cutting through the fragile peace I had built. He raised accusations, claiming that the child might not be Dee's since they did not know about the pregnancy, his voice dripping with disdain. His words pierced the veil of emotional nonchalance I had wrapped around myself, striking straight at my heart. I wondered if he spoke out of malice, deliberately seeking to hurt me, or if he truly believed what he was saying. I wished, more than anything, that Dee was there to stand by me, to defend me, to prove to his family that Tanya was his child. But Dee was gone, and I was left to face the storm alone.

Yet, I refused to let his words define me or my daughter. I did not need to prove anything to anyone. The truth was evident in Tanya's face, in the way she carried pieces of her father within her. Some accusations are so baseless, so cruel, that they do not deserve a response. I chose silence, not out of weakness, but out of strength. I would not let my daughter's worth be determined by the opinions of those who sought to tear us down. Instead, I focused on building a life for her, a life filled with love and security.

My family became my anchor, their unwavering support holding me up when I felt like crumbling. They reminded me that I was not alone, that I was loved, that I was enough. And Tanya, my precious Tanya, became my source of healing. Though my heart ached knowing that Dee would never hold her, never see her grow, I embraced my role as both mother and father. It was exhausting, balancing work and single parenthood, but every smile, every milestone, every moment of joy made it all worthwhile. She was my reason to keep going, my reminder that even in the darkest times, there is light.

As for Dee's father, I could not help but wonder if his rejection stemmed from something deeper, something uglier. There were whispers that he had tried to claim Dee's financial benefits, only to be blocked by the law. Perhaps his frustration, his anger, was directed at me because he could not have what he wanted. But I refused to let his way of grieving define me. I reached out, tried to build a bridge for the sake of my daughter, but he denied it all. And so, I let it go. I chose to focus on the love that surrounded me, the love that Tanya and I shared.

Life, I have learned, is a tapestry woven from threads of joy and sorrow, triumph and loss. And though the road has been difficult, I am grateful for every twist and turn, for they have brought me to this moment. Tanyaradzwa, my comfort, my joy, my miracle, is proof that even in the darkest times, there is light. She is my reminder that God's promises are true, that His plans are greater than anything I could imagine. And as I hold her in my arms, I know that no matter what comes, we will face it together, with love and faith as our guide.

The world has a way of testing the strength of a woman's spirit, of bending her will until it feels as though it might break. But a woman's spirit is not so easily shattered. It is forged in the fires of adversity, tempered by the storms of life, and polished by the hands of love and loss. I found myself standing at the crossroads of grief and resilience, holding my daughter Tanyaradzwa in my arms, a living testament to the miracles that can emerge from the ashes of despair.

For the sake of Tanya, I reached out once more to Dee's father, my voice trembling with a mixture of hope and trepidation.

I asked for Dee's death certificate, a simple piece of paper that would allow me to obtain a birth certificate for our daughter. It was a request born of necessity, not malice, but his response was as cold and unyielding as stone. He refused, his words sharp and final, cutting through the fragile hope I had dared to nurture. At that moment, I felt the weight of exhaustion settle deep within my bones. I had no more energy to fight, no more strength to push against the wall of his indifference. And so, I made a decision. I would give Tanya my last name, my identity, my legacy. She would carry my name forward, a beacon of light in the darkness. At least I had tried. At least I could say that I had reached out, that I had extended an olive branch, even if it was met with rejection.

The months rolled on, each one marked by the quiet rhythm of life with Tanya. She grew, her laughter filling the spaces where sorrow once lingered, her presence a balm to my wounded heart. But the past has a way of resurfacing, of pulling us back into its depths when we least expect it. In 2022, Dee's friends decided to visit his grave. They hoped to convince his father to allow them to place a tombstone in his memory, a lasting tribute to the man they had loved and lost. They invited me to join them, their voices filled with a quiet determination. They believed that perhaps, in the presence of Dee's resting place, his father might soften, might see the truth of my relationship with his son, and might understand the depth of the love we had shared.

When we arrived, I held onto a fragile hope, a fragile belief that maybe, just Maybe, as my name, his father's heart had thawed. But what I encountered was a devastation I had not prepared for. He refused to acknowledge Tanya, his eyes cold and unyielding as they swept over her. Despite the undeniable resemblance between Dee and our daughter, he dismissed it all, his words laced with a bitterness that cut deep. It was as though I were trying to force a child on him, a child he refused to accept as his son's. I stood there, my heart breaking anew, unable to comprehend the source of such hostility. Where did this anger come from? I asked myself. As I stood there, before Dee's resting place, the weight of his rejection pressing down on me tears streaming down my face as I questioned whether Dee had left me to bear all this pain. Clutching my daughter tightly, I wept, wondering how I could ever visit again if every trip meant confronting this heartache even here, in the place where you rest. How will I show Tanya your final resting place when one day she ask where are you? I was hurt to the core; my heart felt heavy and shattered into pieces. I went home with a broken heart.

4

LONELINESS, THE QUIET COMPANION

oneliness became my quiet companion, a shadow that followed me through the days and nights, not because I lacked people around me, but because I lacked understanding. It was a loneliness that no crowd could dispel, no conversation could soothe. It was the loneliness of being unseen, unheard, in a world that moved too quickly, too impatiently, for the pace of my grief. No one seemed to grasp that grief does not come with a deadline that it does not bow to the ticking of a clock or the turning of a calendar. There was no expiration date on love, so why should there be one on mourning? Why should the world demand that I pack away my sorrow like a winter coat when spring arrives, as if it were something I could simply shed when the seasons changed?

I felt, in those moments, like a stranger in my own life, walking among people who had forgotten that Dee and I did not end our relationship—God did. Our love was not a choice we unmade; it was a bond severed by forces beyond our control. And yet, the world acted as though my grief were a choice, as though I could decide, one morning, to wake up and be done with it. But how could I be done with him when my heart still beat with the rhythm of his name? When every breath I took carried the weight of his absence? I still loved him the same way he had loved me until his last breath, with a fierceness that defied reason, a tenderness that defied time. And that love did not die with him; it lived on, a flame that refused to be extinguished, even in the face of his absence.

I could not always explain it, this ache that sat in my chest like a stone, this emptiness that no amount of distraction could fill. I did not have the words to make them understand, to make them see that grief was not a wound that could be stitched up and forgotten. It was a presence, a living thing that moved through me, shaping my days and colouring my nights. It was in the way I reached for him in my sleep, only to wake to an empty bed. It was in the way I heard his laughter in the wind, saw his smile in the sunlight, felt his touch in the warmth of a blanket. It was in the way I carried him with me, always, even as the world moved on.

And so, I walked the road of grief alone, my footsteps echoing in the silence of my heart. I could not pretend he had never existed, could not erase him from my life just to make others comfortable. To do so would have been a betrayal, not just of him, but of me, of the love we had shared, of the life we had built together. And so, I kept on doing what my heartfelt, even when it meant walking against the tide, even when it meant carrying a weight that no one else could see.

But eventually, I realized that I could not carry that weight forever. I had to make an effort to heal, not for the sake of the world, but for the sake of my health, for the sake of Tanya, my precious daughter, who deserved a mother who was whole, who was present, and who was alive in every sense of the word. And so, I began the slow, painful process of healing, not because I wanted to forget him, but because I wanted to honour him, to live a life that would make him proud.

5

INHERITANCE OF MEMORIES

G rief is a universal human experience, yet it is often misunderstood, misrepresented, and mistimed. We have all heard the clichés, the well-meaning but hollow platitudes that are meant to comfort but often only wound. "Time heals all wounds," they say, as if time were a magician, capable of erasing pain with the wave of a wand. "Just move on," they urge, as if grief were a place you could leave behind, like a town you pass through on a road trip. "It's been long enough," they chide, as if grief were a race with a finish line, as if there were a timeline for love, for loss, for healing.

But what if I were to tell you that grief does not work that way? That it is not a straight path, but a winding road, full of twists and turns, ups and downs, moments of clarity and moments of confusion? What if I were to tell you that grief is not something you can "get over" or "move on" from, but something you must carry with you, like a stone in your pocket, a weight that becomes a part of you, shaping you, changing you, teaching you?

As someone who has been navigating this path for over three years, since my husband's passing, I have come to understand that grief is not a journey with a clear beginning and end. It is not a problem to be solved or a puzzle to be figured out. It is a constant companion, a reminder of what you have lost, but also of what you have loved. And love, true love, does not end with death. It lives on, in the memories you carry, in the stories you tell, in the way you live your life.

I realized that grief is not a uniform experience. It does not follow a set path, nor does it adhere to a timeline. For me, grief was a storm that lingered, weaving itself into the fabric of my everyday life. It was there in the quiet moments, in the laughter of my daughter, in the memories that surfaced unbidden. But not everyone understood this. To some, it seemed that I had been grieving for far too long. They whispered among themselves, their voices filled with a mixture of concern and impatience. "She should have moved on by now," they would say, as if grief were a task to be completed, a box to be checked off. But grief is not so easily tamed. It is unpredictable, a force of nature that ebbs and flows, sometimes gentle, sometimes overwhelming. It does not move on a schedule, nor does it fade on command. And yet, the people around me seemed to think that I should have "healed" by now, that I should have forgotten the pain of losing Dee less than five years ago.

When Dee was still with us, he had a way of making every moment special. Every time I felt sick, every Valentine's Day, every Mother's Day, every birthday, every Christmas, he would celebrate with me, his love expressed in the form of special anytime cards. Those cards were more than just pieces of paper; they were tangible expressions of his love, his way of telling me that I was cherished, that I was enough. But one day, when I wanted to read them, to feel his presence in the words he had written, I discovered that they were gone. My family, with the best of intentions, had thrown them away without my knowledge. I was hurt, not just by the loss of the cards, but by the fact that they had not even told me. Those cards were my connection to Dee, a way to feel his love even in his absence. I would have gone back to them, read them, and smiled, not cried, because of the sweet messages they carried.

My own family, with their well-meaning advice, urged me to move on from my grief. They wanted me to stop talking about Dee, stop sharing posts about him, stop mourning him so publicly. "You need to let him rest in peace," they would say, as if my love for him was somehow disturbing his peace. They even suggested that if I kept suffering, he would come back to me, but I would leave our daughter behind to suffer. As if grieving for him was a taboo, a sin to be avoided. But how could I forget him when every day, I saw his face in our daughter's? She had his eyes, his expressions, even his quiet way of observing the world. To ask me to stop thinking about him was like asking me to erase the very presence of him that lived on in our child. I would often joke with them, saying, "Do you want me to swallow Tanya back into my ovaries?" It was a dark humour, a way to deflect the pain of their words, but it also carried a truth. Tanya was a part of Dee, a part of me, a living reminder of the love we had shared.

I tried. I did. I attempted to "move on" in the way they wanted. I tried to open myself up to the idea of love again, to let someone new into my heart. But it never felt right. It felt forced, unnatural, as if I were playing a role that wasn't meant for me. I stepped back, realizing that their version of happiness did not align with what I felt. I knew how I wanted to be loved, I knew what love was, I had been there, and I knew how to be loved right. And so, I chose to honour the love as a gift and wait for right time.

But here is the thing, People cannot see grief. They cannot touch it, taste it, or smell it. It is an invisible weight, a burden that you carry alone, because others do not understand it. They cannot comprehend why you "can't" just "move on," why you "can't" just "get over it." They do not grasp that grief is not something you can hurry along, something you can add to your daily planner, something you can check off your to-do list. It is not a task to be completed, but a journey to be lived. Friends and family, those who are meant to support you, can often be the ones to lead you astray. They mean well, of course, but they do not always understand. They do not understand where you are coming from, the depth of your pain, the weight of your loss. And they do not understand where you are going, the uncertain road ahead, and the journey you must take to find your way back to yourself.

The truth is, grief is not something you can put into a neat little box and store away. It is a living, breathing entity that evolves with you, changes with you, grows with you. It is not static, but dynamic, shifting and changing as you move through life. And the only way out of pain is to go through it, not around it. You cannot avoid it, cannot sidestep it, and cannot pretend it does not exist.

You must face it, head-on, with courage and honesty, even when it hurts.

I have learned this lesson the hard way. I have confronted my grief head-on, often by looking at pictures of Dee, watching videos of us together, and reading through our old chats. It is painful, yes, but it is also cathartic. It is a way for me to process my emotions, to work through the pain, to honour the love we shared. It is not easy, but it is necessary. And it has helped. It has helped me to heal, to find a new sense of normal, to carry his memory with me in a way that is not debilitating, but empowering.

I still miss him of course. I still wish he were here with me, still wish I could hear his voice, feel his touch, see his smile. But the pain is no longer overwhelming. It is no longer all-consuming. It is a part of me, but it does not define me. It is a reminder of what I have lost, but also of what I have loved, of what I am capable of loving.

Grief is simply something that must be navigated, one step at a time. And we need to understand that grief is not a sign of a broken mind, but of a broken heart. It is not a one-size-fits-all experience, but a deeply personal journey, unique to each individual. People often assume that to heal, you need to "move on" and "love again." But that is not always the case. You can still get married again, still find happiness again, but that does not mean you have forgotten about the loss of a loved one. Love is not a finite resource; it is infinite, boundless, capable of expanding to include new people, new experiences, new joys, without erasing the old. I have often felt like no one understands this journey, like everyone has something to say that is not based on reality. But I have learned that it is okay to feel that way. It is okay to be angry, to be sad, and to be confused and it is okay to not have all the answers.

And so, I walk this path, not with the expectation of reaching a destination, but with the understanding that the journey itself is the destination. I carry my grief with me, not as a burden, but as a reminder of the love I have known, the love I have lost, and the love that still lives on in me. And in that, I find my peace, my healing, and my legacy.

For me, the journey through grief has been long and arduous, a winding road that stretches endlessly before me, with no clear destination in sight. There have been times when I thought I would never stop crying, when the tears flowed like a river, carving deep grooves into the landscape of my soul. There were moments when the pain was so sharp, so all-consuming, that I thought it would never fade, that it would be my constant companion until the end of my days. But slowly, imperceptibly, the tears began to dry, the pain began to dull, and I learned to navigate the treacherous waters of my grief.

I stopped crying, but that did not mean I stopped grieving. Grief is not something that can be measured in tears or in words. It is not something that can be quantified or contained. And just because I no longer cry does not mean I have forgotten. Not posting about him, not talking about him does not mean I have erased him from my heart. And posting about him, talking about him does not mean I am failing to accept the reality that he is gone. It simply means that I am honouring him, that I am keeping his memory alive, and that I am refusing to let the world forget the love we shared.

To those who are supporting someone who is grieving, I want to say this: be patient. Be understanding. Do not try to rush the process or offer clichéd advice. Just be present. Just listen. Grief is a journey that is difficult to navigate, but with patience, understanding, and support, it is possible to find a way through. Grief is a reminder that love never dies, even when the people we love do. It is a testament to the depth of our connections, to the bonds that tie us to one another, even in death.

6

A TURNING POINT

Tanya's birth was a turning point in the grief that I was experiencing. Her coming into this world granted me a reprieve, a moment of respite from the relentless storm of sorrow that had consumed me. For the first time since Dee passed away, I felt the void he had left being filled, not completely, but enough to bring a glimmer of light into the darkness. I felt the ice that had encased my heart melting away, bringing a new warmth and happiness to my soul. I always secretly smile when I look at her, even in my darkest moments. I knew, the moment I set my eyes on her, that my healing process had just begun.

I started to pick myself up from the dire state I was in. I knew I had to focus, for the sake of the precious life that Dee and I had created. Tanya became a new purpose for my existence, a reason to keep going, to keep fighting, to keep living. Every time I felt low, every time I felt depressed, I would simply remember that Dee had not left me alone. He had left me a daughter, his copycat, my legacy. In her, I saw so much of him—his eyes, his smile, his quiet way of observing the world. She was a living reminder of the love we had shared, a love that had not died with him but lived on in her.

I found myself getting a newfound vigour to live, to take care of my daughter, my only ray of light in a pitch-black world. But with that newfound purpose came a new fear, a fear that gripped me in its icy claws and refused to let go. I was so afraid of losing her, especially after she was born prematurely, that I spent days without sleeping in the hospital. I do not know where all the fear was coming from. Maybe it was because I had almost lost her when she was not yet born, because I had carried her through a pregnancy marked by grief and uncertainty. Whatever the reason, the fear was real, and it was paralyzing.

7

A TEST OF FAITH

I had requested to be transferred from Harare back to Masvingo ZB Bank branch, so that I could be close to my family. It turned out to be one of the best decisions I had ever made. Being around my family helped me to lighten the burden and to ease the weight of grief. They were my anchor in the storm, my safe harbour in the tempest. With them, I could share moments of laughter, moments of joy, even as I continued to navigate the waves of sorrow that threatened to pull me under.

But even with their support, there were moments when the grief would resurface, when the pain would become too much to bear. I remember one incident in particular, a moment that almost threw me into an abyss of depression from which I would never emerge, even in a thousand years. Tanya was a month old, and I had gone out, at the instruction of my mother, to refresh my mind and take a breath of fresh air. My mother had quickly taken on the role of comforter, my only anchor in the storm. She was taking care of Tanya and me, because at that time, I was too weak emotionally and physically to do it on my own.

It had been a long time since I had been out alone, without feeling an emptiness that made me claustrophobic. I left Tanya with my mother, while I took a moment for myself. But on this day, I experienced a pain that seemed to deepen the already raw grief of losing my husband. My daughter, after a bath, was sleeping peacefully, a picture of innocence and vulnerability. She was the centre of a mystery that still haunts me, a moment that tested my faith and reminded me of just how fragile life can be.

In a room that should have offered solace, there was nothing but a solitary super king bed. And yet, inexplicably, my two young nephews, who were at home that day, managed to scale that bed. It is still a mystery to me how a three-year-old could accomplish such a feat, especially when even a five-year-old might have found it impossible to climb that bed. As they crept into the room, these little beings produced hair combs from who knows where. In their innocent mischief, they began to comb my daughter's hair, their small fingers handling something so delicate and precious.

But what was meant to be a harmless act turned tragic when the combs, in their unknown origin and unbidden intrusion, caused damage to her tender face. That day, my heart broke in a way that words can scarcely capture. I was left with questions about where those combs had come from, about the strange ability of those children to defy what I believed were the boundaries of their world, and about the inexplicable circumstances that led to this wound on my daughter's innocent skin. Each unanswered query added to the layers of sorrow, marking that moment as the most painful experience I had endured since my husband's passing.

This incident stands as a symbol of life's unpredictable cruelty. When I first saw my daughter's face after the incident, I could barely recognize my child. The swelling was so severe that her tiny features seemed to disappear beneath the bruises. Where her eyes should have been, there were only thin slits, just enough to hint that they were there. Her nose looked smaller than ever, lost in the puffy skin around it, and her cheeks were so swollen they merged into the rest of her face. The worst was her mouth—her upper lip was so enlarged that it covered the lower one entirely, leaving just a glimpse of where her sweet baby lips should have been.

Seeing her in that condition was heart-breaking in ways I can hardly describe. She was just a fragile new life, who had already endured an inexplicable trauma. I remember feeling an ache in my chest so deep it rivalled the grief I felt after losing my husband. It was a moment that tested my faith, reminding me of just how vulnerable life can be. Yet, amid the fear and sorrow, I held onto hope—hope that she would heal completely, that the innocence of her early days would be restored, even if it left behind a scar in my heart.

Even though she recovered, the fear of losing her multiplied. She was like a treasure that my husband had left for me, a precious gift that I could not bear to lose. The incident left me shaken to the core, and I became even more protective of Tanya, fearing the worst. I watched over her with a vigilance that bordered on obsession, determined to keep her safe, to shield her from the cruelties of the world.

8

A REVELATION: TURNING PAIN INTO PURPOSE

There were moments—oh, there were moments—when the memories would come flooding in, a tidal wave of emotion that threatened to drown me, to suffocate me beneath the weight of what had been and what could never be again. It was during those times, when I would see people receiving gifts from their loved ones, their faces alight with joy, their hearts full of the warmth of connection, that I felt the sharpest sting of loss. My Dee, was buried deep under a pile of black soil, his voice silenced, his touch gone, his presence reduced to memories that sometimes felt more like ghosts than echoes of the past.

Sometimes the memories would be so intense, so vivid, that they would rip open wounds I thought had begun to heal. I would find myself gasping for air, clutching at the fragments of a life that had been torn apart, wondering how I could possibly go on when the pain was so raw, so relentless. I realized, in those moments, that what was happening was not good for me. The grief, the sorrow, the longing—it was consuming me, eating away at the edges of my soul, leaving me hollow and broken. I knew I had to do something, but I did not know what. How do you heal a heart that has been shattered? How do you find peace when the world feels like a cruel and unforgiving place?

I was receiving counselling, of course. I had sought help from professionals, from my church, from my family and friends. They offered words of comfort, of wisdom, of hope. But still, the pain lingered, a shadow that followed me wherever I went. I realized that maybe, just maybe, I needed closure. Not the kind of closure that comes from forgetting or moving on, but the kind that comes from honouring what had been, from finding a way to say goodbye to the dreams that had died with Dee.

One day in April 2022 as I was going through some papers, I came across my collection of "anytime" cards from Dee. These were little tokens of love, surprises he would leave for me, each one a reminder of the depth of his affection, the sweetness of his heart. As I sifted through them, my hands trembling, my eyes blurred with tears, I felt a fresh wave of pain crash over me. Each card was a piece of him, a piece of us, a piece of a life that had been so full of love and promise.

And then, my hands landed on a brochure for the Great Zimbabwe Ruins in Masvingo, a place we had visited together with his close friends, a place that had held so much meaning for us. The brochure advertised wedding and event bookings, and as I stared at it, I felt a sharp, searing pain in my chest. It was a reminder of the wedding we had planned but never had, a dream that was stolen by cruel fate.

We were supposed to be married on September 25, 2021. It was a date we had chosen carefully, a date that had been etched into our hearts, and a date that was supposed to mark the beginning of a new chapter in our lives. We had wanted to wed before my baby bump became too obvious, before the world could see the physical manifestation of the love we had shared. But that day never came. The ceremony we had envisioned, and the vows we were supposed to exchange, the celebration we had dreamed of, all of it had been taken from us, leaving behind a gaping wound that refused to heal.

That memory of our lives remained open, unfinished, haunting me in ways I could not escape. The memories of the wedding we had planned would come back to me in flashes, vivid and painful. I would remember the venue we had chosen, the navy blue and champagne colour scheme, the cake we had designed, every little detail we had carefully planned. What had once been a beautiful dream now felt like a cruel mockery, a reminder of what could have been, of what should have been.

As I sat there, surrounded by the remnants of our love, I felt the tears begin to flow, hot and relentless. But then, in the midst of my grief, a thought interrupted the sorrow, a spark of something that felt almost like hope. Instead of allowing the pain to consume me, I wondered if I could channel it into something meaningful, something that would honour Dee's memory in a way that brought joy rather than pain.

It was in that moment that I had a revelation. I needed to find a way to bring closure to that dream, to lay it to rest, if I ever hoped to heal from the pain of love and weddings. I needed to find a way to celebrate the love we had shared, to honour the life we had built together, even if it was in a different way than we had planned.

And so, I began to think of what I could do. The Great Zimbabwe Ruins, brochure had brought back so many memories. I thought of a wonderful couple from church, Mr. and Mrs. Magara, who were about to celebrate a milestone anniversary. They had been married for many years, their love a testament to the enduring power of commitment and devotion. With the help of my pastor, I approached them with a heartfelt proposal. I wanted to host a small anniversary celebration for them, attended by members of my church, New Life International Ministries. I wanted to pour my heart and soul into the preparations, to create an event that would honour their love in the same way I had wanted to honour mine with Dee. I had bought what they were going to wear, I offered to bake a cake for the occasion, decorated in the navy blue and champagne colours Dee and I had chosen for our wedding.

When they accepted, I saw tears of joy in their eyes, and at that moment, I knew I had made the right decision. This was not just about them; it was about me, about finding a way to heal, to find closure, to honour the love I had lost. I did the preparations, and with the unwavering support of my family, the event took shape.

It became a labour of love, a way for me to channel my grief into something beautiful, something meaningful. With each step, I felt my grief slowly lifting, the weight of sorrow being replaced by a sense of purpose, of hope. Instead of being weighed down by the pain of what I had lost, I found healing in giving. Instead of envying couples in love, I chose to celebrate love, just as Dee and I would have.

The anniversary day celebrations were held on May 30, 2022, a day that would forever be etched in my memory as a turning point in my journey through grief. It was beautiful, a tapestry of emotions woven together with threads of joy, sorrow, and hope. The air was filled with the soft hum of laughter, the gentle rustle of fabric, and the sweet scent of flowers. The venue, adorned with navy blue and champagne decorations, was a reflection of the love Dee and I had dreamed of celebrating. But this time, it was not our love being honoured—it was the enduring love of Mr. and Mrs. Magara, a couple whose commitment to each other had stood the test of time.

As I stood there, watching them renew their vows, I felt a surge of emotions that I could not quite name. There was joy, yes, but also a deep, aching sadness, a reminder of what I had lost. Yet, amidst the sorrow, there was also a sense of peace, a quiet understanding that love, true love, never dies. It transforms, it evolves, but it never fades. Seeing the joy on their faces, the way they looked at each other with such tenderness and devotion, reminded me that life is precious, that love is a gift to be cherished, even when it is no longer within our grasp.

In that moment, I realized that I had found a way to heal, a way to honour Dee's memory and legacy. I had taken the pain of my loss and channelled it into something beautiful, something that celebrated love rather than mourning its absence. I watched the couple dance together, their faces alight with joy. I felt a sense of closure, a sense of peace that I had not felt in a long time. I choose to celebrate love, in choosing to honour his memory in a way that brought joy rather than pain, I found a way to move forward, to find healing, to find hope. The Magaras' family attended, their presence was a testament to the power of community, of shared joy and shared sorrow. Seeing their happiness, their gratitude, made me feel as though a part of my dream had been fulfilled, albeit in a different way. To this day, I am forever grateful to that couple for allowing me to turn my sorrow into something beautiful, for giving me the opportunity to find healing in the act of giving.

That experience showed me that even in the darkest times, there is always the potential for love, joy, and transformation. Grief is not just about what we have lost; it is also about what we can give. It is about finding ways to honour the love we have known, to celebrate it, to share it with others. And in doing so, we find healing, we find peace, we find hope. Before the anniversary, the thought of attending marriage-related gatherings had felt like too much to bear. It was a painful reminder of what I had lost, of the dreams that had been shattered. But on that day, something shifted within me. I felt a sense of peace, a quiet acceptance that allowed me to remember Dee without being overwhelmed by grief. It was as though the act of celebrating love, of honouring it in others, had opened a door within my heart, allowing me to step into a new chapter of my life. Up to today if I see a marriage-related gathering, if I see people in love, I bless them.

As time passed, I began to feel a sense of clarity, a renewed sense of purpose. The counselling I had received was working, helping me to navigate the complex emotions that came with grief.

And then there was Tanya, my precious daughter, who had become my inspiration, my reason to keep going. She had not only filled the void left by Dee's absence but had also taken his place in my heart, becoming a living reminder of the love we had shared. My family, too, had played a crucial role in my healing. There were times when I had been difficult to handle, when my grief had pushed their patience to the limit, but they had never wavered in their support. They had stood by me, offering comfort and understanding when I needed it most.

9

CROSSING OCEANS, CARRYING MEMORIES

In March 2023, I made the difficult decision to move to the UK in search of a better life for Tanya. It was not an easy choice. Leaving behind my daughter, who was only a year and two months old, as well as my entire family, felt like tearing a piece of my heart away. But I knew it was necessary. I wanted to provide Tanya with opportunities that I had never had, to give her a future filled with promise and possibility. My sister was already working in the UK, and her presence offered a glimmer of comfort, but the thought of stepping into a new place, filled with unfamiliar faces and unfamiliar customs, filled me with a sense of trepidation.

More than that, it felt as though I was leaving Dee behind. His memories were vivid, etched into the fabric of my being, and the idea of crossing the oceans, of being thousands of kilometres away from the places where we had shared our brief but beautiful time together, made me fear that distance would somehow erase those memories. But deep down, I knew that nothing could ever change that.

Despite the emotions that swirled within me, I knew I had to go. Better opportunities were waiting for me, and I wanted to provide Tanya with the best life possible. At that point, my purpose felt clear, ensuring Tanya's well-being was all that mattered. But beyond that, another reason weighed on my heart. I had an undeniable urge to care for others, perhaps as a way of making peace with the fact that I never got to care for Dee the way I had hoped. If I could make a difference in someone else's life, if I could offer love and care where it was needed, maybe it would bring me a sense of fulfilment, a sense of closure. At the same time, it was an opportunity for me to pursue my career and build a future, not just for myself but for my daughter as well.

Settling in the UK proved to be easier than I had anticipated. There was a community of Zimbabweans who had already made their home there, and they were quick to welcome me into their social circles. We were like one giant family, united by our Zimbabwean roots and, in some cases, similar life experiences. We would laugh and share stories of our lives back home, reminiscing about the places we had left behind and the dreams that had brought us to this new land. For a moment, I felt a sense of belonging, a connection to something larger than myself.

But amidst the laughter and camaraderie, I knew I had to stay focused on my purpose for moving to the UK. I could not let the weight of memories hold me back. I had come here to build a better future for Tanya, to create a life filled with love and opportunity. And so, I threw myself into my work as a care worker, finding solace in the act of caring for others. It was not always easy, there were moments of exhaustion, of doubt, of longing for the familiar, but I reminded myself of why I had come here, of the love that had brought me to this place.

Moving to the UK was not just a physical journey; it was a journey of the heart, a journey of healing and hope. It was a way for me to honour Dee's memory, to create a life that would make him proud. And as I look to the future, I am filled with a sense of possibility, of promise. I know that there will be challenges ahead, but I also know that I have the strength to face them, the love to sustain me, and the hope to carry me forward.

This newfound clarity of mind, this poignant focus, was like a gentle breeze that swept through the corridors of my soul, clearing away the cobwebs of grief and regret. For the first time in what felt like an eternity, I was ready to let my past slide. Not to forget it, no, never to forget it but to release the tight grip it had on my heart. I would keep the memories, hold them close like precious treasures, but I would no longer allow them to chain me to a place of sorrow. It was hard to let Dee go, harder than I had ever imagined, but every time I thought of him, I found myself smiling instead of weeping. His memory, once a source of unbearable pain, had become a beacon of light, a reminder of the love we had shared, the life we had built together.

I immersed myself wholeheartedly into my work, filling my mind with positivity and focusing on building a better life. It was a conscious choice, a deliberate effort to move forward, to create something new from the ashes of what had been. But just as I began to feel a sense of stability, a sense of purpose, my thoughts turned to Tanya, my precious jewel. And with those thoughts came a deep, aching longing that I could not ignore.

I began to miss Tanya deeply, her absence a void that no amount of work or distraction could fill. She was my only tangible connection to Dee, the physical manifestation of the love we had created together. And the day I left for the UK, it felt as though I had severed that bond, as though I had left a piece of my heart behind. A wave of sadness and loneliness crashed over me, stirring emotions I had tried to bury beneath a mask of professionalism at work. My body felt weak, my spirit weary, and I feared falling back into the depression I had fought so hard to escape.

The weight of my emotions became too much to bear, and in July 2023, just a few months after leaving, I flew back to Zimbabwe. I needed to see Tanya, to hold her in my arms, to reconnect with my family, and to free myself from the grip of loneliness that was consuming me. The moment I saw her, a sense of relief washed over me, but it was short-lived. The reality of our separation hit me hard, like a blow to the chest. She did not recognize me.

When I tried to hold her, she pulled away, her tiny body stiff with uncertainty, her eyes wide with confusion. She stared at me as if she were trying to place a familiar face from a distant memory, as if she were trying to reconcile the woman before her with the mother she had known. In that moment, my heart shattered. The bond I had thought unbreakable had been strained, stretched thin by the distance and time that had separated us.

Tanya remained distant, needing time to warm up to me again. I could see the hesitation in her eyes, the way she would glance at me, then look away, as if unsure of whom I was. It was a painful process, watching her slowly piece together the fragments of our relationship, trying to remember the mother who had been there for her in the beginning. Just as she finally started to recognize me, just as she was beginning to accept me again, it was time for me to leave. The cruel irony of it all weighed heavily on me as I prepared to return to work in the UK.

When I returned to the UK, I thought I would feel better, that the visit would have eased the ache in my heart. But instead, things worsened. The migraines that had plagued me for years became more severe, and their intensity unbearable. I struggled to sleep, my mind racing with thoughts of Tanya, of Dee, of the life I had left behind. Even the simplest tasks became difficult as my memory started to fail me, my thoughts scattered and unfocused. I felt overwhelmed, lost in a sea of emotions that I could not navigate.

Feeling desperate for relief, I sought medical help, hoping for some kind of solution, some kind of reprieve. After an assessment, my GP referred me to a mental health practitioner. The referral took me aback. Did I need a mental health evaluation? The thought unsettled me, stirring a mix of fear and confusion. They suspected I might be suicidal, but suicide was the farthest thing from my mind. I wanted to live for Tanya, for the legacy Dee and I had built, for the future we had dreamed of. They concluded I had a severe mild depression. But the weight of my emotions, the depth of my despair, had become too much to bear alone.

I knew I needed to do something to fix this, to find a way to heal, to reclaim the life I had worked so hard to build. In November 2023, I flew back to Zimbabwe once again. My family questioned my decision, their voices filled with concern. Why did I keep returning home instead of saving money and investing in my future? But at that point, I was drowning in depression, the weight of my emotions pulling me under. The thought of not going back to the UK crossed my mind more than once. I had even resigned from my workplace, the job that had once been a source of stability and purpose.

Being with Tanya, however, gave me strength. She reminded me why I had to keep going, why I had to fight, why I had to find a way to heal. Motherhood had given me a resilience I never knew I had, a strength that came from the depths of my soul. Tanya was my reason, my purpose, my light in the darkness. And as I held her in my arms, as I watched her smile, as I felt her tiny hands reach for me, I knew that I could not give up. I had to keep going, for her, for Dee, for the life we had built together.

The journey through grief, through loss, through separation, is not an easy one. It is a path filled with twists and turns, with moments of light and moments of darkness. But through it all, I have learned that love is the thread that binds us together, the force that carries us forward. Tanya's presence, the love of my family and friends it has been my anchor, my guiding light.

After much thought, after nights spent staring at the ceiling, wrestling with the weight of my choices, I realized I could not walk away from the opportunity I had worked so hard for. The UK had become more than just a place of work; it was a symbol of resilience, of the life I was trying to build for Tanya, for myself, for the legacy Dee and I had dreamed of. And so, with a heart heavy yet determined, I returned to the UK. This time, I was armed not just with my will to survive, but with a plan to thrive. I attended therapy sessions, allowing myself to be vulnerable, to unpack the grief that had settled in the corners of my soul. I took medication to help manage the depression that had threatened to consume me, and I embraced another job opportunity, a new chapter in a story that was still being written.

Through it all, one truth became clear, shining like a beacon in the storm, there was only one way for me to truly heal. I needed Tanya. I needed her laughter, her tiny hands, her wide-eyed wonder. I needed her presence, her warmth, her love. She was not just my daughter; she was my lifeline, my connection to Dee, my reason to keep going. And so, I made the decision that would change everything. I would bring Tanya to live with me.

I quickly made arrangements for Tanya and my mother to join me in the UK. When they arrived in March 2024, it felt as though a missing piece of my soul had been restored. Tanya's presence was like a balm to my wounded heart, her laughter a melody that chased away the shadows that had lingered for so long. She had a therapeutic effect on me, her innocence and joy soothing the pain I had been carrying. My mother's support was equally invaluable. She was my rock, my anchor, her unwavering love and strength a reminder that no matter how old we get or what we go through, a mother's love remains a source of comfort and stability.

I felt incredibly fortunate to have her by my side during one of the most difficult periods of my life. Her presence was a gift, her wisdom a guiding light. She not only helped with childcare but also provided the emotional support I so desperately needed. Together, we navigated the challenges of this new life, finding solace in each other's company, in the shared love for Tanya, in the memories of Dee that bound us together.

While having Tanya with me was a blessing, I found myself torn over whether she should stay in the UK or return to Zimbabwe with my mother. The challenges of balancing work and childcare were immense, the weight of responsibility heavy on my shoulders. I worried about the impact of uprooting her life, about the sacrifices I would have to make, about the future I was trying to build for her. After much deliberation, after countless sleepless nights and tearful conversations of not knowing what to do, I finally chose to have her stay with me. It was not an easy choice, but deep down, I knew that having her close was what my heart needed. She is my reason, my purpose, my light in the darkness. And so, I made the decision to keep her with me, to build a life together, no matter how difficult the road ahead might be.

10

OPENING MY HEART

As time passed, I had accepted that Dee was truly gone. The finality of his absence, once a source of unbearable pain, became a quiet truth that I carried with me. And with that acceptance came a glimmer of hope, a faint whisper that maybe, I could open my heart to love again. In 2024, nearly three years after his passing, my friends introduced me to someone who, to my astonishment, felt like a reflection of Dee. It was almost eerie, the way he spoke, his facial expressions, his body language, his voice, even his handwriting and personal style mirrored my late husband's. The only noticeable difference was his height. For a fleeting moment, it felt as though fate had handed me a second chance at the love I had lost.

Drawn in by the familiarity, I found myself connecting with him, allowing myself to believe that perhaps this was a sign, a gift from the universe. But the illusion did not last. I soon realized that it was not him I was drawn to; it was the echoes of Dee in him. The resemblance, instead of bringing comfort, became a painful reminder that no one could ever truly replace the love I had lost.

Deep down, I had been unconsciously expecting him to step into Dee's place, to fill a void too vast to ever be filled. Our connection, though strong, was not enough to overcome the reality of our circumstances, and we eventually parted on good terms.

The experience taught me a valuable lesson, that healing is not about replacing what has been lost, but about finding a way to carry it with you, to honour it, to let it shape you without consuming you. I could love again, not as a replacement, but as a continuation of the journey we had begun together. And so, I move forward, not with the expectation of forgetting, but with the hope of healing. I move forward with Tanya by my side, her laughter a reminder that life is precious, that love is a gift to be cherished. This fleeting encounter with a man who mirrored the love I had lost, taught me a lesson as profound as it was painful. While memories and similarities may bring temporary solace, like a fleeting breeze that cools the skin on a sweltering day, they can never truly substitute for the love and bond that once existed.

11

A JOURNEY OF STRENGTH: THE SISTERHOOD OF WIDOWS

As I try to navigate the complexities of being a single mother, I am struck by the lessons I have learned, the truths I have uncovered, the strength I have discovered within myself. I have learned that being strong is not a trait you are born with, but a choice you make, day after day, in the face of setbacks that threaten to overwhelm you. It is a decision to rise, to fight, to keep going, even when the world feels heavy, even when the path ahead is shrouded in uncertainty.

I have managed to brave the turbulent waters of widowhood, a title no woman prays for, a role thrust upon me by the cruel hand of fate. Widowhood is not a label I wear with pride, but it is one I wear with dignity, because it is a part of my story, a part of the journey that has shaped me into the woman I am today. It is a journey of loss, yes, but also of resilience, of courage, of hope.

In my journey, I was privileged to find a space where I could share my pain, where I could learn from others walking a similar path. It was a WhatsApp group called Widows Cote, a gathering of young and old women, all bound by a common tragedy—the loss of their husbands. In this group, I found a sisterhood, a community of women who understood the depth of my pain, who had felt the same ache in their hearts, the same emptiness in their lives.

In this group, I heard countless stories of heartbreak, stories that went beyond the grief of losing a spouse. Women spoke of being deserted by their husband's families, of being cast out by people who once called them *muroora* (daughter-in-law) but now saw them as outsiders. They were no longer welcome in the homes they had built their lives around, no longer part of the families they had loved and served. Some were cut off entirely, as if they had never existed, as if their love, their sacrifices, their very presence had been erased.

One recurring pain we shared was the fear and suspicion we faced from society, especially from other women. Widows, it seemed, were seen as a threat, as if losing a husband automatically meant we were searching for someone else's. Married women kept their distance, their eyes filled with a mixture of pity and suspicion, afraid that we might set our sights on their husbands simply because we were alone. It was as if widowhood was equated with desperation, as if we had suddenly become predators simply because life had taken a turn we never anticipated.

There was also the belief that a widow was incapable, that she could not build, create, or succeed without a man beside her. Society expected that certain achievements—from buying a home to raising well-mannered children—were only possible within a marriage. If a widow dared to accomplish what a married couple did, she was met with doubt and criticism, as if her success was somehow illegitimate, as if her strength was a threat to the status quo.

But I refuse to accept this narrative. I refuse to be defined by society's narrow expectations, by its fears and prejudices. A widow is not a broken woman. She is not a threat. She is not helpless. A widow is simply a woman who has loved and lost. Nothing more, and nothing less. She is a woman who has known the depth of love, the joy of connection, the pain of separation. She is a woman who carries her loss with grace, who finds strength in the face of adversity, who builds a life for herself and her children, not out of desperation, but out of determination.

A widow is a woman who rises, who fights, and who perseveres. She is a woman who knows the value of love, not because she has lost it, but because she has felt it. She is a woman who understands that life is not defined by what is taken from us, but by what we choose to do with what remains. She is a woman who refuses to be silenced, who refuses to be diminished, and who refuses to be anything less than extraordinary.

And so, I carry my widowhood with me, not as a badge of shame, but as a testament to the love I have known, the loss I have endured, the resilience I have discovered. I carry it in the way I hold Tanya close, in the way I build a life for us, in the way I refuse to let society's expectations define me. I carry it with grace, because to do otherwise would be to dishonour the love Dee and I shared, the life we built, the dreams we dreamed.

Widowhood is not a sentence, but a story, a story of love, a story of loss, and a story of resilience. It is a story that is still being written, a story that I am proud to be a part of. And as I move forward, I do so with the knowledge that I am not alone, that I am part of a sisterhood of women who have loved and lost, who have risen and fought, who have carried their voids with grace. Together, we are redefining what it means to be a widow, one story at a time.

She is a mother, just like any other. She wakes up in the morning, her eyes heavy with the weight of dreams interrupted, yet her spirit unyielding. She prepares meals, not just to nourish tiny bodies, but to feed the souls of the children who look to her for everything. She nurtures, she guides, she loves with a fierceness that defies the odds stacked against her. She carries the weight of both mother and father on her shoulders, a burden she did not choose but one she bears with a grace that is nothing short of miraculous. She is a widow, a title she never asked for, a role she never imagined, yet one she has embraced with a strength that is both humbling and awe-inspiring.

I believe that being a widow is, in its way, a blessing in disguise. Not because of the pain, not because of the loneliness, not because of the countless nights spent staring at the ceiling, wondering how to piece together a life that feels shattered. No, it is a blessing because of the strength it forces you to uncover within yourself. It is a blessing because it reveals the depths of your resilience, the power of your spirit, the unyielding force of your love. It is a blessing because it teaches you that you are capable of more than you ever imagined that you can rise from the ashes of despair and build something beautiful, something lasting and something true.

Before this tragedy, I was a queen. I was cared for, protected, cherished. I never needed to worry about the simple things like changing a bulb, fixing a leak, making tough decisions alone. Dee was my partner, my protector, my confidant. He was the one who held my hand through the storms, who stood by my side when the world felt too heavy to bear. But now, he is gone, and I am left to navigate this world alone. Now, I know that no one is coming to do these things for me. It is either I sit in the dark, or I change the bulb myself. It is either I let the leak destroy my home, or I pick up the tools and fix it. It is either I crumble under the weight of my grief, or I rise, stronger and more determined than ever.

This is the truth of widowhood. It does not mean weakness; it means self-reliance. It does not mean defeat; it means discovery. It means uncovering parts of yourself you never knew existed, parts that are strong, capable, and resilient. It means realizing that you can do what you never thought possible, that you can face challenges you never imagined, that you can build a life for yourself and your children, even when the world feels like it is against you. It means knowing, deep in your soul, that God saw you fit to raise your children alone because He knew you had the strength to do so. He knew you were capable, He knew you were resilient, He knew you were a warrior.

To every widow who has been made to feel small, invisible, or incapable, know this: you are more than your loss. You are more than the pain, more than the grief, more than the loneliness. You are a survivor, a warrior, a builder of legacies. You are a woman who has loved deeply, lost profoundly, and risen from the ashes with a strength that is nothing short of miraculous. You are a mother, a protector, a guide. You are a beacon of hope, a testament to resilience, a living example of the power of the human spirit.

And no one, not society, not the whispers of judgment, not even your fears, can take that away from you. You are not defined by your loss, but by how you choose to carry it. You are not defined by the absence of your partner, but by the presence of your love, your strength, your determination. You are not defined by the challenges you face, but by the courage with which you face them. You are a widow, yes, but you are also so much more. You are a force to be reckoned with, a light in the darkness, a testament to the power of love and resilience. This group of widows has reminded me that, even in the face of loss, there is still so much to live for. They have taught me that, while I may be a widow, I am also a mother, a protector, a guide. I am a woman who has faced the unimaginable and emerged stronger, more determined, more resilient

And as I move forward, I do so with the knowledge that I am not alone, that I am part of a sisterhood of women who have loved and lost, who have risen and fought, who have carried their voids with grace. Together, we are redefining what it means to be a widow, one story at a time. Together, we are building legacies of love, of strength, of resilience. Together, we are proving that, while the road may be difficult, it is also filled with moments of joy, of love, of hope. And in that, we find our strength, and our purpose.

I managed to pick myself up from the fires of dead stars, from the ashes of a life that once felt whole. I dusted myself off, wiped away the tears, and decided to live not just for myself, but for Tanya. She is my reason, and my purpose. She is the living embodiment of the love Dee and I shared, the love that continues to live on, even in his absence. And now, as I wait for the challenges that may lie ahead, I hold on to the faith and hope of a better life for my child. I hold on to the belief that, no matter what comes our way, we will face it together, with love, with strength, with resilience. Amidst the sorrow, I have found moments of hope and resilience. I have found joy in the laughter of my daughter, in the milestones she reaches, in the love we share. She is a reminder that life goes on, that there is still beauty to be found in the world.

12

REVEALING THE TRUTHS WE BURY

Surprisingly, children have a way of revealing truths we try to bury, truths we tuck away in the corners of our hearts, hoping they will fade with time. Their innocence, their unfiltered honesty, lays bare the things we struggle to put into words, the things we fear to confront. My daughter, Tanya, in her own small yet profound way, showed me the depth of what she was missing before she could even fully understand it herself. She became a mirror, reflecting the ache of absence, the longing for a presence that was no longer there. And in her innocent questions, her hopeful smiles, her quiet tears, I saw the truth of her little heart's yearning, a truth that broke me and healed me all at once.

It started subtly, as these things often do. Every time I spoke with a man over the phone, Tanya would perk up, her face lighting up with excitement, her voice filled with a hope that was both beautiful and heart-breaking. "Mama, ndidad here?" ("Is that Dad?"), she would ask, her words a mix of curiosity and longing. At first, I brushed it off as childlike curiosity, a simple misunderstanding. She was too young to fully grasp the concept of loss, too innocent to understand that the voice on the other end of the phone could never be her father's. But then, it became a pattern, a recurring theme in her little world, and I could no longer ignore the depth of what she was feeling.

If a male visited, her reaction was always the same, her face bright with hope, as she greeted them with a beaming smile. She would run to me, her tiny feet pattering against the floor, her voice filled with excitement. "Dad vauya!" ("Dad is here!") She would exclaim. At first, I thought she was merely mimicking those around her. Back in Zimbabwe, she spent time with my brother's daughters, who called their father "dad," and I assumed she was just copying them, as children often do. She even called my brother her "dad" till date. I realized it was not just mimicry. It was longing. It was a silent, persistent yearning for something she had been denied before she even had the chance to know it. It was the ache of a child who, in her own innocent way, was searching for a father she would never truly have.

One day, the truth of her little heart's ache became painfully clear. In our home, we had a simple mug, one that belonged to my friend, the one I shared a flat with. It was not special in any way, except for the fact that it had a printed image of a male figure. No specific face, just a generic silhouette of a man. To Tanya, that was enough. She clung to it, her tiny hands gripping the mug as if it were a lifeline, tears welling in her eyes as she insisted, "Ndoda cup ina daddy." "I want the cup with daddy."

It broke me.

In that moment, I fully understood that my daughter was not just playing pretend. She was searching, reaching for something she would never truly have. She was creating a father in places where he did not exist—in voices over the phone, in the faces of strangers, in a simple image on a mug. In her innocent mind, dad was not just a person. Dad was a presence, a feeling, a role she longed to fill in any way she could. And there is no pain, quite like watching your child yearn for something you cannot give her. I could hold her, love her, reassure her, but I could never be the dad she so desperately sought. I could never fill the void left by Dee's absence, no matter how much I wished I could.

And so, I did the only thing I could do. I let her call them "dad." I let her hold onto that mug. I let her find comfort in the illusion, hoping that one day, she would understand that while her father may not be here, she is and always will be deeply loved. Because even in his absence, his love still lingers. It lingers in the way I hold her, in the way I speak of him, in the way I tell her that God is in our story, even in the spaces we wish were filled. It lingers in the memories we share, in the love we carry, in the life we are building together.

13

GRIEVING AT MY OWN PACE

One of the most important lessons I have learned is that it is okay to cry. Crying is not a sign of weakness; it is a release, a way to let out the emotions that can otherwise consume you. Emotional tears contain more stress hormones, and if suppressed, they can lead to stress, anxiety, and depression. So, I cry when I need to. I let the tears flow, not as a sign of defeat, but as a way to cleanse my soul, to release the pain, to make space for healing. And with each tear, I feel a little lighter, a little stronger, a little more at peace.

I have also found hope through therapy, through the support of loved ones, and through the inner strength I never knew I had. Therapy has been a lifeline, a safe space where I can unpack my emotions, where I can confront the pain and find ways to move forward. The support of my family and friends has been a source of comfort, a reminder that I am not alone, that there are people who care for me, who love me, who are walking this journey with me.

And then there is my inner strength, the resilience that has carried me through the darkest times. It is a strength I did not know I had, a strength that has been forged in the fires of grief, tempered by the challenges of single motherhood, and polished by the love I have for Tanya. It is a strength that reminds me that, no matter how difficult the road may be, I have the power to keep going, to keep fighting, to keep loving.

Writing this book has been a therapeutic process, a way to process my emotions, to find solace in sharing my story. It has allowed me to reflect on the journey that brought me to this point, to honour the love I shared with Dee, to celebrate the life we built together, and to acknowledge the pain of his absence. Writing has been a way to heal, to find meaning in the loss, to create something beautiful from the ashes of despair.

There are still moments when the pain resurfaces, when the grief feels fresh and raw. There are days when I allow myself to feel the weight of my loss, to sit with the pain, to let it wash over me like a wave. In those moments, I allow myself to grieve. I allow myself to feel the emotions, to cry, to remember. But I also remind myself that grief is not the end of the story. It is a part of the journey, a part of the healing process. I still remember Dee, his laughter, his smile, the way he held me, the way he loved me. I miss him deeply, achingly, in a way that words can scarcely capture. But I have also learned to cherish the memories we shared, to hold them close like precious treasures, to let them bring me comfort and joy. And as I move forward, I find joy in the little things, the way Tanya closes her tiny eyes when she is laughing, the way she smile at me and say "I love you mama," the way she hugs me tight and doesn't want me to leave her, the way she kisses me goodbyes when I am leaving for work.

14

A HEART FULL OF THANKS

Thank you for walking this journey with me, for holding my hand through the storms, for standing by my side when the world felt too heavy to bear. Thank you for listening to my story, for sharing in my pain, for celebrating my triumphs. I hope my story has brought you comfort, a reminder that you are not alone, that there are others who have walked this path, who have faced the darkness and emerged into the light. I hope it has inspired you, reminded you of the power of the human spirit, of the strength that lies within each of us, waiting to be uncovered. And I hope it has given you hope, a reminder that even in the face of loss, life continues, and with it, the promise of a brighter tomorrow.

This journey of healing, of building a life after loss, is not an easy one. It is a path filled with twists and turns, with moments of light and moments of darkness. But through it all, I have learned that love is the thread that binds us together, the force that carries us forward. Dee's love, Tanya's presence, the love of my family and friends, it has been my anchor, my guiding light. There are still moments when the pain resurfaces, when the grief feels fresh and raw but God is in the story.